PAULINE LECLERC

Conservatory graduate pianist

30 PIANO SHEET MUSIC FOR BEGINNERS

THIS BOOK BELONGS TO

Foreword

This repertoire of simplified classical and folk music is intended for students who are new to the piano, but who already knows how to read music and place their fingers on the instrument.

This is not a learning method, but a sheet music support, classified from the simplest to the most complicated piece. It is designed to help you grow from beginner to intermediate pianist.

Classical music is a great way to learn the piano, however, it is not always enjoyed by novice pianists.

This is why I only chose well-known and short pieces in order to combine enjoyement and improvement.

This is the secret to progress quickly!

Musically yours,

Pauline Leclerc

CONTENTS

Canon in D

Johann Pachelbel

Ode to Joy

Ludwig van Beethoven

Moonlight Sonata

Ludwig van Beethoven

Spring - The Four Seasons

Antonio Vivaldi

Piano Sonata N° 8

Ludwig Van Beethoven

The Blue Danube

Johann Strauss Jr.

Symphony N° 5

Ludwig van Beethoven

Swan Lake

Pyotr Ilyich Tchaikovsky

Gymnopedie n° 1

Erik Satie

13

Für Elise

Ludwig van Beethoven

Minuet in F Major

Wolfgang Amadeus Mozart

Minuet in G Major

Johann Sebastian Bach

A Little Night Music

Wolfgang Amadeus Mozart

Sleeping Beauty

Pyotr Ilyich Tchaikovsky

Clair de Lune

Claude Debussy

Greensleeves

Unknown composer

Symphony N° 40 in G Minor

Wolfgang Amadeus Mozart

2

The Old French Song

Pyotr Ilyich Tchaikovsky

Nocturne Op. 9 N° 2

Frédéric Chopin

Piano Sonata N° 11

Wolfgang Amadeus Mozart

Dance of the Sugar Plum Fairy

Pyotr Ilyich Tchaikovsky

Dreams of Love

Franz Listz

Morning Mood

Edvard Grieg

Waltz Op. 69 N° 2

Frédéric Chopin

Turkish March

Wolfgang Amadeus Mozart

Waltz in A Minor

Frédéric Chopin

Fantasia

George Frideric Handel

Prelude N° 1 in C Major

Johann Sebastian Bach

The Peddlers

Russian folk song

G Minor

Johann Sebastian Bach

Manufactured by Amazon.ca
Bolton, ON

29144905R00028